The Dreadful Truth

The Dreadful Truth

Canadian Crime

Ted Staunton

**Illustrations by
Remie Geoffroi**

Formac Publishing Company Limited
Halifax, Nova Scotia

Formac Publishing Company Limited acknowledges the support of the
Culture Division, Nova Scotia Department of Tourism, Culture and
Heritage. We acknowledge the financial support of the Government of
Canada through the Book Publishing Industry Development Program
(BPIDP) for our publishing activities.

We acknowledge the support of the Canada Council for the Arts for
our publishing program.

Library and Archives Canada Cataloguing in Publication

Staunton, Ted, 1956-
      Canadian crime / Ted Staunton ; illustrated by Remie Geoffroi.

(The dreadful truth; 4)
ISBN-13: 978-0-88780-705-3   ISBN-10: 0-88780-705-4

      1. Crime—Canada—History—Juvenile literature. I. Geoffroi,
Remie II. Title. III. Series: Dreadful truth

HV6803.S68 2006   j364.971   C2006-904374-4

Formac Publishing Company Limited
5502 Atlantic Street
Halifax, Nova Scotia B3H 1G4
www.formac.ca

Printed and bound in Canada

Contents

Pioneers of Crime

Canadians have invented many things, from those you'd
expect, like snowmobiles, to those you wouldn't, like basketball
and better screwdrivers. Still, despite a long and close
relationship with it, we cannot claim to have invented crime.
Just like our own Robertson screwdriver, though, we have given
it a few new twists.

Crime here goes back a long, long way, to before there even
was a Canada. The first recorded offence dates from 1542,
when a member of Sieur de Roberval's tiny settlement was
accused of theft. There couldn't have been a lot to steal; maybe
that's why they hanged him.

Among the many honest, hardworking people who came to
Canada to make a better life, some were driven to crime by
sheer desperation. Others lost their way by drinking too much
back when liquor was one of the few comforts around. Then
there were the honestly *dis*honest folks, many, unfortunately,
just as hardworking. Some were sent here when other
governments cleaned house — petty criminals were forced to
become some of our earliest settlers, in almost suicidal
conditions. Ladies of the night were shipped to New France as

prospective brides. For other criminals, Canada meant fresh pickings, or a safe place to go until things cooled off back home. And a few crooks were here because, well, they were running the place.

Under the usually peaceful surface of Canadian life ran a rough and tumble current as tough as the times. It could bubble up in startling ways. In Halifax, a military town, things got so wild that arsonists tried to burn down the firehouse. Pirates roved. So did government press gangs that tried to kidnap you into the navy. Lonely country byways could make good places for a robbery. Bloody feuds and hatreds could erupt. Bribery, corruption, and heavy drinking were ways of life.

While there were courts and laws, there were no police, no detectives and no crime science. Keeping the peace was something the whole community had to look after, sometimes with surprising results.

Inevitably, crime moved west with settlement and in the true pioneer spirit, it kept up with changing times: the first attempted train robbery in North America took place near London, Ontario.

Since then we've come up with endless variations on crime and punishment. Forgers, fools, tricksters, traitors, thieves, and cold-blooded killers stumble through these pages on their bizarre journeys, some funny, some savage, some sad, and some still shrouded in mystery.

Luckily, we've also come up with better ways of coping with crime and criminals. Some of that story is told here too. So, if any of the spectacularly bad activities in this book sound like good ones to you, keep in mind a couple of other Canadian inventions we'll talk about: the world's first crime science lab, and the RCMP.

The Big One

Murder is the ultimate crime. Deliberately taking another person's life is so grim and mysterious to most of us that killers seem as if they must come from another planet. Not so. An American crime reporter has famously observed that the person most likely to murder you is probably sitting across the breakfast table.

Before this spoils your morning, understand what the reporter meant: statistics show that most murders are "crimes of passion." The killer has acted out of character in a highly emotional moment, attacking someone they know well. And there's usually more to it than hogging the toaster — often a tangle of love and hate, not to mention greed, religion, politics, and mental illness.

Some murders are interesting for their *why*. In 1893, for example, John Hooper probably would have gotten away with killing his wife if he hadn't insisted that her already-buried body be exhumed for embalming. This couldn't be done without an inquest, which eventually led to his twenty-five-year sentence. Why in the world did he want her embalmed?

Then again, the *how* or *who* of the murder are sometimes eyebrow raisers. In 1900, Minnie McGee of Charlottetown poisoned her family with sulphur scraped from the ends of matches.

Then there was Henry James Smith, who killed his wife by hitting her on the head with the family Bible (Bibles were heavy in 1890). As a bonus, at his execution Smith called for time out to confess he was also a bigamist, having deserted a wife in England when he came to Canada.

And sometimes, how the case was solved is the grabber. In 1859, Professor Henry Crofts of Toronto used a test for arsenic poisoning that helped convict Dr. W.H. King of murdering his wife. Arsenic, odourless and tasteless, had been such a popular and undetectable poison that its nickname was "inheritance powder." Crofts' testimony was the first scientific evidence in a Canadian murder case. It probably changed more than a few secret plans.

The most notorious Canadian murders stick out like headstones in the graveyard of the past. Here are some that still dot the landscape.

Keeping Ahead

Samuel de Champlain was the target of one of Canada's first intended murders. A dispute over the fur trade in the early 1600s put the new governor in conflict with rival traders and, business being business, they decided to kill him. Learning about the plan, Champlain had the leader of the plotters strangled. For good measure, the man's head was then cut off and stuck on a pole for public viewing. Three other conspirators were sentenced to the gallows in France; the rest were pardoned — to show there were no hard feelings. There was, however, that head on a pole for everyone to look at.

The Widow Corriveau

Marie Corriveau's husbands slept so soundly they never woke up. Her first died in his sleep in 1760, and it was whispered around St. Vallier, Quebec, that Marie had poured molten lead into his ear while he snoozed. Her second husband lasted two-and-a-half years before expiring in *his* sleep, this time because Marie whacked him to death with a pitchfork. Then she dragged him to the stable and tucked him under a horse to make it seem as if he'd been kicked to death.

Oddly, this clever ruse didn't fool anyone, and Marie and her father were charged with murder. Dad gallantly took the blame and was sentenced to death, at which point he changed his mind and blamed Marie. She was hanged instead.

(She was lucky. By 1763 the British had captured Quebec. Under English law, she could have been burned at the stake.)

Yo-Ho-Ho

Okay, so you've got Pirates of the Caribbean, but *Pirates of the St. Lawrence*? Yup, the less glamorous Gulf of St. Lawrence was home to a number of pirates, including some particularly bloody husband-and wife-teams (who presumably got along better than the Corriveaus). In 1809, for example, Mrs. Edward Jordan lent a hand when her husband captured a trading schooner. She tried to kill the captain with a boat hook while her helpmate dispatched two of the crew with an axe. The captain leapt overboard and was picked up by another ship. Because the captain swam, Mr. Jordan swung — from the gibbet in Halifax.

Even more vicious were Maria Lindsey and Eric Cobham, whose motto was "Dead cats don't mew," and whose policy was "Sink the ship and murder everyone." The psychopathic Lindsey poisoned a ship's crew, sewed the men in sacks and had them dropped overboard, and used prisoners for target practice. Eventually she and Cobham retired to France as wealthy gentry. He became a magistrate and she a drug addict. After Lindsey's death, Cobham wrote a tell-all memoir, which his by-then respectable family tried to hide.

Business Is Business

Cutthroat competition is not always just a phrase. In the rivalry between the Hudson's Bay Company and the North West Company, it was a way of life — or death. From 1783 to 1821, the two businesses literally fought it out over the fur trade, conducting vicious raids on each other's isolated trading posts. Traders were beaten and murdered, furs and supplies stolen, and buildings burned. Twenty-one people were massacred when Métis traders (encouraged by the North West Company) attacked the Hudson's Bay outpost at the Red River. When the two companies were finally amalgamated in 1821, it was found that the North West traders had thirty-two cannons in their west coast arsenal, just in case.

Fighting Words

In June 1833, John Wilson and Robert Lyon paced off the distance and shot at each other in a dispute over the affections of Elizabeth Hughes. Lyon was killed and Wilson was acquitted of murder. He then married Elizabeth Hughes and became a lawyer in London, Ontario.

Duels were one way of settling a feud, or dispute, in our past and they pop up as late as the 1870s. Most feuds were not as short or clear cut as that of Wilson and Lyon. They were often bloodier, as well, as first one side then the other added to a list of wrongs so long that what started things hardly mattered any more. The most famous Canadian feud was between the rambunctious Donnelly family and their neighbours along the Roman Line near Lucan, Ontario, in the mid-1800s. Like many in the area, the Donnellys had migrated from Tipperary, Ireland, bringing old-country enmities with them. When one of them fought and killed a neighbour at a barn raising, the trouble began all over again. The ugly tit-for-tat battle dragged on for years. It culminated in a midnight raid on the Donnelly homestead in which five members of the family were murdered. The Donnellys were so despised that the killers, easily identified, were acquitted of the crime. One of them was the local constable.

Thompson, Gunner

Nova Scotia's Ben Thompson personified the Wild West gunman, with a lifetime average of more than one killing a year over a long career as a gunslinger. As a young man in the 1860s he headed to the U.S. and served with the Confederate South in the Civil War. Then he hired on as a mercenary with the Mexican army. From there, Ben headed up to Kansas, where he alternated between work as a sheriff or an outlaw, depending on the demand. (The main qualification for both

jobs was a willingness to shoot people.) After his brother killed
the sheriff in Ellsworth, Kansas, Ben single-handedly held off a
lynch mob. Moving on to Abilene, he was a rival of Wild Bill
Hickok for a time, heading south after Hickok was gunned
down in a poker game. Thompson was finally ambushed too,
in a theatre in San Antonio, Texas, in 1884. By then, he had
killed well over thirty men.

The Assassination of D'Arcy McGee

Thomas D'Arcy McGee, one of the fathers of Confederation,
was the target of Canada's first political assassination.
Immensely popular, his funeral in Montreal was the occasion
for a huge outpouring of public grief.

Before coming to North America, McGee had been involved
in the rebellious politics of his native Ireland. He thought he had
left all that behind, but it wouldn't let him go. At two o'clock
a.m. on April 7, 1868, just after speaking in a late sitting of
Parliament, he was shot point-blank in the back of the neck as
he bent to unlock the front door of his Ottawa boarding house.
McGee died instantly. Patrick James Whelan, a militant
Irishman, was arrested soon after, carrying a revolver from
which one bullet had been fired. Based on this and a few other
scraps of circumstantial evidence (there were no witnesses,
and this was long before ballistics tests) Whelan was convicted
and hanged. For many years after, there was controversy over
whether he was wrongly convicted (see *Unsolved Mysteries*).

The Big Benwell Case

The Benwell murder case of 1890 was a sensation in Canada and
England. It highlighted the perils of far-off lands at a time when

many Britons were thinking of emigrating. As well, the details of the case and its cracking could have come straight from a then-newfangled kind of entertainment: the detective story.

In 1889, a Mr. and Mrs. Birchall went to England, looking for young men from wealthy families who might be interested in becoming partners in a horse farm near Niagara Falls. The opportunity attracted both Reginald Pelly and Frederick Benwell, who returned to Canada with the Birchalls in early 1890 to look at the property. Their families would forward the necessary cash if they liked it.

When they reached Ontario, Benwell suddenly left the group. Birchall told Pelly that the other man had had to return home. They went on to Niagara Falls.

Meanwhile, two men clearing trees in the Blenheim Swamp near Woodstock, Ontario, stumbled on a man's body. It had two bullet holes in the back of the head. All identification had been stripped away, right down to the labels in the clothing.

Ontario's chief detective, John Wilson Murray, was called in. A faint trail of bloodstains showed Murray that the body had been dragged to its hiding place. Backtracking, he found the trampled ground of the murder scene. Two days of searching on his hands and knees turned up nothing but a cigar holder half-buried in the mud. It was embossed with the initials *FWB*. Murray publicized the initials and a photo of the dead man in the newspapers, hoping they would help identify the victim.

It worked. The Birchalls arrived and identified Benwell's body, saying they had met him casually on a ship returning from England. Sensing something was wrong, Murray kept an eye on Mrs. Birchall as he asked her husband more questions. He was sure from her reactions that Birchall was lying. He arrested them both the next day.

It didn't take long to turn up passengers from the ship, not to mention Pelly, who was still waiting in Niagara Falls. The Englishman, increasingly suspicious, still hadn't seen the farm. It seemed that Birchall had kept inviting him walking instead — by the cliffs near Niagara Falls.

There was no farm. The Birchalls had lured the men to Canada to kill them. Their unsuspecting families in England would have received letters saying the two were happily settled and doing well — and to please send the investment money. Instead, Pelly survived, the Birchalls did not, and Murray became internationally famous as a kind of real-life Sherlock Holmes.

Body of Evidence

Evelyn Dick hated boredom. By the time she married John Dick, a streetcar motorman, in 1945, she'd already had quite a bit of

excitement. Working as an upscale "party girl" while still living at home in Hamilton, Ontario, Evelyn had not only the high life, but two young children, one of whom never seemed to be around.

Things didn't get quieter after the wedding. Evelyn refused to live with her new husband, being busy with another boyfriend. When John Dick found out, there was a huge quarrel between him and Evelyn and her parents. Threats were made.

Not long after, John disappeared. Ten days later his torso was found on a hiking trail outside the city. Police searched Evelyn's place for the rest of him and found instead the body of a baby in a cement-filled suitcase. It was her missing child.

Evelyn, her parents, and the boyfriend were tried for John Dick's murder. Evelyn was convicted, but then acquitted on appeal. Instead, she was convicted of manslaughter in the death of her baby son.

Out of the Blue

On September 9, 1949, a bomb exploded forty minutes into a CPAir DC-3 flight out of Quebec City, killing all twenty-three people on board. It was Canada's first mass murder, a terrible foretaste of a crime that has become a symbol of international terrorism. As it turned out, this first case had nothing to do with terrorism, except for the killers' sickening contempt for human life.

Investigators traced the cargo on board. This led them to, among others, a woman named Marguerite Pitre, who had shipped a package on the flight. Pitre, a mother of two, at first seemed an unlikely suspect. Nothing obviously connected her to the tragedy, except that the wife of a friend, Albert Guay, was on board. Pitre owed Guay $600 she couldn't afford to repay. And Guay, it turned out, was romancing a woman who worked with Pitre. He wanted to be rid of his wife. He'd told Pitre he'd kill the debt if she killed his wife.

Pitre bought dynamite and, together with her brother and Guay, made a bomb. She took it to the airport and shipped it on the flight. All three were convicted of murder. Marguerite Pitre was hanged on January 9, 1953.

It's a Steal

Don't Knock It...

If you look at lists of criminal convictions from the past, you'll see that one of the most frequently punished crimes is theft.

Some stealing was probably for sheer survival: laundry from clotheslines, loaves of bread, small change, tobacco. With other things it's harder to tell. Door knockers, for example: Montreal underwent a rash of door knocker thefts in 1815. It's hard to imagine a big market for hot door knockers. Were they sold as scrap metal? Torn off by picky decorators? Or was it a prank, like today's light-fingered lifting of lawn ornaments? We'll never know.

In the early days of settlement, the theft of animals, which were essential to survival, was as serious a crime as murder and was often punished by death. As communities grew and the range of things to steal expanded, crooks got more creative. Banks and trains and steamboats became profitable targets. Consumer society was on its way.

The Family Business

William Johnston ran a family business. The business was armed robbery.

Born in Quebec in 1782, Johnston married an American and settled with his wife near Kingston. During the War of 1812, when Canada was at war with his wife's homeland, he was suspected of helping the U.S. He was jailed and his property was seized. Escaping, the embittered Johnston became a pirate and smuggler, roaming the Thousand Islands in the St. Lawrence River and preying on Canadian targets.

The man was thorough. On one mail-coach robbery, he took all the passengers' clothing as well as their money. Johnston himself dressed for success with six pistols and a Bowie knife. He also had a special boat made for his river work. Powered by twelve oars, it could carry twenty passengers (plus loot), yet was light enough to be carried by two men.

By the 1830s, the whole family was in the gang, and by the time of the 1837 Rebellions they were ready for their biggest score. As Canadian rebels fled to the States and formed "patriot" groups for cross-border raids (see *Us Against Them*), Johnston joined right in. Calling himself "Admiral," he captured the Canadian passenger steamer *Sir Robert Peel*, burned it, and made off with a $100,000 haul. Then, with a ragtag group,

he tried to invade Canada at Prescott. Since Canada and the U.S. weren't at war, this embarrassed the U.S. too. They put him in an American jail for a year to cool off, where he was looked after in grand style by his daughter Kate.

Johnston died in 1870, aged 88 and unrepentant, boasting that he'd cost Canada a lot more than what was taken from him in 1812.

Better than a Three-Ring Circus

Whenever P.T. Barnum's famous circus rolled into town, it arrived in a grand parade. The music and spectacle were great for drumming up business for the circus. On August 1, 1876, it gave some other folks a chance too. As the circus blared through Halifax, everyone crowded the streets to watch, including the tellers of the Bank of Nova Scotia. In the ten minutes the bank employees were outside, some slick-as-Barnum entrepreneurs slipped inside and emptied the tills of $22,000. The suspects were never convicted. No one knows if they caught the show.

All Aboard

Canada was proud to host the first attempted train robbery in North America in 1856. Two men were caught trying to pry up a rail on the Great Western RR line, just outside London, Ontario. It was a long, tough job, and it pointed up a problem of train robbing: first, you have to find a way to stop the train.

Going for another first, the Great Western also hosted Canada's first successful train robbery in 1874. Five men disguised in, of all things, Ku Klux Klan robes looted a train between Toronto and Port Credit, making off with $45,000.

The McLean Gang

Allan, Charlie, and Archie McLean were twenty-five, seventeen and fifteen when their B.C. crime spree ended in 1879.
The children of a Native mother and a white father, the boys were poor, unschooled, and unloved. Their father was a man who hated Natives even more than he hated everyone else. He was shot — despite his habit of wearing a steel breastplate under his shirt — leaving the boys on their own.

Accepted by neither their mother's people nor their father's, the McLean kids stuck together, doing odd jobs on ranches to get by. Soon they were stealing and fighting. In 1877, Charlie got three months in jail for biting off the end of a man's nose in a brawl. He broke out with another boy named Alex Hare, who joined Charlie and his brothers to form an outlaw gang. Archie was twelve at the time.

With no police to stop them, the McLean Gang terrorized southern B.C. for two years, rustling, robbing, and beating their victims. Finally, they stole a horse from a rancher named Palmer. He came after them with the local constable and a posse. Guns were fired. The unarmed constable tried to calm everyone. The brothers shot him, then stabbed him to death.

The posse rode back for reinforcements. The McLeans stripped the dead constable of his coat and boots and rode off as well, Charlie nursing a wound. They headed for a nearby

Native reserve, hoping to get help. On the way, they murdered a sheepherder, then robbed a rancher, flipping a coin to decide whether or not to kill him.

At the reserve, the luckless brothers found that the Natives didn't want them either. The posse returned to find the McLean Gang holed up in a cabin. The gang surrendered after a five-day standoff. They were beaten badly and thrown into jail on Christmas day, 1879. Despite pleas for mercy because of Archie's age and their grim lives, the brothers were hanged on January 31, 1881.

The Nose that Knows

"Flat Nose" George Curry hailed from Prince Edward Island, but he heard and followed the call of the Wild West. George's talents for robbing banks, people, and trains earned him a spot in the Wild Bunch. Also known as the Hole-in-the-Wall Gang, after their mountain hideout, the gang was led by Butch Cassidy and the Sundance Kid. The Hole-in-the-Wall Gang robbed their way across the western U.S. in the 1890s until Butch and Sundance fled to South America, probably dying there in a shootout. George ended up flat as his nose, blown away by a Utah posse in 1900.

Foxy Grandpa

Old Bill Edwards looked like somebody's granddad. He was charming — courtly even — and his ranching neighbours in the Nicola Valley of B.C. were happy to keep an eye on his

place when he had to be away for a few weeks in September 1904, November 1905, and May 1906.

Oddly, these were also the dates of three major train robberies, two in B.C. and one in the northwestern U.S. Despite a $15,000 reward, most folks were happy the train robbers had gotten away. Westerners hated the CPR for its land grabbing and high rates. So when the bandits, posing as prospectors, were nabbed, and kindly Bill Edwards turned out to be their leader, his neighbours rallied around him as a kind of modern-day Robin Hood.

Edwards' real name was Bill Miner. Born in 1847 in Kentucky, he was robbing stagecoaches from the time he was a teenager, regularly in and out of jail, including San Quentin. He was known as "The Gentleman Bandit" for his unfailing good manners while sticking you up. By 1881 he was in San Quentin again, this time for twenty-five years.

When he got out in 1901 he was fifty-four, the last of the old-time outlaws. Stagecoaches were long gone. Bill changed with the times and started robbing trains.

Now, at the age of fifty-nine, he pulled another twenty-five years in the New Westminster Penitentiary. Saying he'd finally learned his lesson, he won over the warden's daughter by reading the Bible with her — until he escaped under the fence surrounding the prison brickyard.

The public cheered Bill's vanishing act, which lasted until 1911, when he was nabbed robbing a train in Georgia. Sentenced to another twenty years, he escaped twice more before dying in custody in 1913. The very last of the Old West died with him.

The Gang that Couldn't Drive Straight

Taking the prize for most inept thieves in Canadian history is a gang of five men who set out from Winnipeg one hot August day in 1921, planning to rob the bank in Elie, Manitoba. Not having a car, they took a taxi, talking out their plan on the way. Too late, they realized the cab driver could hear them. They tied him up, left him in a ditch, and took the taxi.

Unfortunately, they had bad directions. While they got lost, the cabby got free and hopped a train. At the next town, he called the Winnipeg police. Instead of calling their counterparts in Elie, they put a posse together. Meanwhile the crooks had finally reached the bank, robbed it, and headed back for Winnipeg. The police found them just outside the city, still sitting in the taxi. It had broken down.

Booze and Bad Behaviour

Crime has always been thirsty work. Liquor and lawbreaking have snuggled together like a cork in a bottle, from the fur trade to the flappers of the 1920s. Often, drinking has helped people do vicious or foolish things. In some times and places, liquor itself was illegal. Interestingly, this has always made the crime rate go up.

"Water" You Waiting For?

Drinking was a gigantic part of daily life all through Canada's history. In town, the water could well be tainted and beer was the safest substitute. A nickel bought a quart of the stuff,

far stronger than today's brew. Or it bought a "grunt": all the whiskey you could swallow without stopping for a breath. Alcohol was a painkiller for the sick, the secret ingredient in patent medicines. Mixed with water, it was given to babies to help them sleep. It lubricated political meetings. (When the Fathers of Confederation met in Charlottetown they brought $13,000 worth of champagne, in a time when wages averaged a dollar a day.) Above all, it was the Great Escape from lives of hardship, a ticket to forgetfulness anyone could afford.

Or could they? Wages were often drunk away before families were fed. In 1891 an Ontario Royal Commission report said, "Drunkenness does more than any other cause to fill the jails." About one third of all convictions were for drinking. This caused the formation of Temperance societies, groups that tried to have liquor banned. Other people stuck with a more laissez-faire attitude — in the 1830s, one definition of a gentleman was "someone who could afford to be drunk regularly."

Firewater

Alcohol infected the fur trade right from the start.

 Native peoples traded furs to Europeans for many useful things — knives, guns, axes, traps, flint-and-steel sets for starting fires — but the number-one item was liquor.

At first, rum was on offer, but soon traders realized the inexperienced Natives could be fooled with far cheaper concoctions. Grain alcohol was diluted and mixed with sugar or fruit extract, then given an extra zing with "oil of vitriol" (sulphuric acid) to make it seem stronger. Traders called it "high wine"; Natives called it "firewater." They'd spit some into the fire; if the flames blazed up, the drink was strong enough. Not only were the Natives cheated out of the value of their furs, their lives and health were devastated by addiction to the poisonous brew.

Fort Whoop-Up

In 1869, Canada bought the vast area known as the North West from the Hudson's Bay Company. It was mostly uninhabited and undefended, and the government was afraid the U.S. would move in and take over. The American Civil War had ended in 1865 and a lot of unemployed men with guns had headed west. There was a vague semblance of law down in the American West, even if it was thanks to men like Ben Thompson. While Native peoples of the North West had their own customs of justice and codes of behavior, these meant nothing to the cash-hungry traders who headed north to buy their furs. The Hudson's Bay Company had pretty much stopped trading liquor for furs, reasoning that drunken trappers didn't do much work. The new "whisky traders" didn't care.

They built illegal forts as trading posts, and offered their own brand of firewater to the thirsty. The traders' premium blend contained ginger, paint thinner, tobacco juice, laudanum (a powerful narcotic), molasses, pepper, and red ink for color. The trading was done through a wicket in the wall of the fort. Natives weren't allowed inside, since the traders knew that drinking and rifles were a dangerous mix.

The best-known place of this kind was Fort Whoop-Up. Run by Al Hamilton and Johnny Healy, the place made a $50,000 profit in six months, trading rifles and firewater for buffalo hides and pemmican. Natives and buffalo were almost destroyed by the whisky trade, which climaxed in the Cypress Hills Massacre in 1873. Thirteen drunken traders wiped out thirty Assiniboine Natives they suspected of stealing horses.

Canada's response was to form an armed force called the North West Mounted Police (*Police* sounded less threatening than *Rifles*), and send them to deal with the trouble. By the fall of 1874, they reached an empty Fort Whoop-Up. For the whisky traders, desertion was the better part of valour. They were never a problem again. The Mounties liked the fort so much they offered to buy it to use as a post. Hamilton and Healy wanted too much, so instead Fort McLeod was built for the Mounties.

Chain Lightning and Death on Wires

Natives were not the only drinkers cheated on their tipple. The navvies working to build the CPR in the 1880s were even thirstier, but not allowed to drink. Still, enterprising traders found ways to smuggle booze into the work camps. It was packaged as food, or coal oil, or even nitroglycerin. Liquor was

stashed in the boilers of broken locomotives, in the carcasses of dead horses, in the pump organ used for church services. In Regina, a "pregnant" woman toted booze in a rubber bag under her dress, while pushing a carriage that held a baby-sized keg wrapped in a blanket.

The liquor was made from a gallon of alcohol mixed with nine gallons of water and tinted with tea. The gallon of alcohol cost a whisky peddler fifty cents. He'd sell the ten gallons of rotgut at twenty-five cents per one-ounce shot. There are 128 ounces in a gallon. You do the math.

The men called the stuff Chain Lightning, Death on Wires, Tanglefoot, or Forty Rod (a rod was a distance; forty of them were about 200 metres) after how far the stuff would knock you. A few shots of Tanglefoot and the knives and guns tended to come out. Finally, the Mounties had to assign two officers to each camp to keep the peace.

How Dry I Am

By the early 1900s, the Temperance movement was gaining strength. It was an odd time. In Ontario, on a Sunday, it was against the law to buy an ice cream cone or a newspaper, or to play or watch sports. Down in Michigan, high heels were forbidden on Sundays. By 1920, the U.S. had introduced Prohibition, a ban on making and selling liquor. Canada had been "dry" for the last year of World War One as part of the war effort, but manufacturing was started again in 1919.

This is where things got complicated. Making booze was controlled by federal law, but selling it was up to the provinces. Quebec allowed liquor sales. Ontario, among others, didn't. Still, Ottawa wasn't going to give up the money it made on liquor taxes. It was now perfectly legal to make and sell liquor, but only for export.

Canadians leaped into the business of smuggling booze into the U.S.; it was a crime, but only on the American side of the border. By July of 1920, smugglers were moving a thousand cases of whisky a day from Windsor, across the Detroit River, to the U.S. They used boats in summer. In winter, they drove jalopies across the ice. (You'd use a cheap old car so the loss wasn't too great if the ice broke.) The area was known as the Windsor-Detroit Funnel.

Elsewhere on the Great Lakes, rumrunners would load up their boats and head out across the open water. If you were daring and had a big fishing boat, you could make more in a week of smuggling than you would in eight months of work as a fisherman.

Still, the job was tough and dangerous, especially for those

trying to make a run in winter. Ben Kerr, known as the King of the Rumrunners, died in a winter storm in 1929. His boat, the *Pollywog*, could carry 100 cases of whisky and a crew of three, and still do 40 knots an hour. The *Pollywog* was only yards from shore, but there was so much ice it couldn't land. Kerr and a crewman drowned as the boat smashed to pieces in the frigid lake.

And if the lake didn't get you, there was always the chance of a shootout with the U.S. Coast Guard, or the perils of dealing with American gangsters like Al Capone, waiting for your cargo on the other side.

Thirsty Work

Ontarians were as thirsty as their American neighbours. It wasn't long before enterprising smugglers began "short-circuiting" their cargoes back into Canada for bootleggers to sell under the counter or in illegal saloons called "speakeasies." They'd order liquor from a distiller and have it sent by train to a port on Lake Ontario for "export." On the Canada Customs form, they'd write that they were sailing to Mexico or Cuba. Then they'd chug off across the lake and double back when they were out of sight, landing the booze at some out-of-the-way place on the Canadian side. Some boats left for "Cuba" four times a day.

There were other ways to go the distance for a drink. Quebec, for example, was "wet," and motor trips to Montreal became popular. Airplanes were also used. Brian Peck, the pilot of the first airmail flight in Canada, barely got off the ground on that maiden trip: his plane was overloaded with cases of contraband scotch.

Or you could get liquor with a doctor's — or veterinarian's — prescription. One doctor wrote 1,244 prescriptions in a single month, including nearly 250 in a single day. Each prescription was good for one quart of whisky. In May 1921, the Ontario government imposed a limit on doctors of fifty prescriptions a month. Finally, late in 1923, the government realized Prohibition wasn't working. By 1925, Ontarians could buy beer — at 4.4 percent alcohol; it had been 9 percent before. By 1927, you could buy one quart of liquor a day at a government store. The drought was over, here. In the U.S. it lasted until 1933.

Rocco and Bessie

Canada's version of Al Capone was a team. Rocco Perri met Bessie Starkman in 1912, when he took a room in the Toronto boarding house she ran with her husband. They ran off together, despite the fact that Rocco was so poor he couldn't afford shoes.

What they both had was ambition. Rocco found work in a bakery. By 1916 he was heading a bookmaking/numbers racket. Meanwhile, Bessie was running a brothel out of their house and selling whisky on the side. Next they bought a neighbourhood grocery in Hamilton, Ontario, and started bootlegging in volume. Soon they were living in a nineteen-room mansion, lavishly entertaining a heady mixture of mobsters and high society. Bessie, the brains of the operation, kept business humming by bribing corrupt officials — and literally killing the competition. Rocco was implicated in ordering seventeen murders. By the mid '20s Rocco, no shrinking violet, was calling himself King of the Bootleggers.

Eventually Rocco and Bessie were both called to testify before a government commission about the liquor trade. Bessie found it hard to explain her claim of having a net worth of only ninety-eight dollars. Charged with perjury, Bessie got off and Rocco served six months.

In 1930, Bessie paid a higher price, blasted by shotguns in her Hamilton garage. Rocco threw her a true gangland funeral, at which pickpockets apparently made out like, ahem, bandits. It was Rocco's last hurrah. By 1933, he couldn't afford twenty dollars for car repairs. By 1944, he didn't need to drive himself anyway. Someone took him for a ride.

Going Overboard for the Lord

Not all the misbehaving was done by the "wets." In 1920, there was none drier than Reverend J.O.L. Spracklin, a Methodist minister in Sandwich (near Windsor), Ontario.

Reverend Spracklin had been a childhood rival of Babe Trumble, who grew up to own a speakeasy. In the summer of 1920, Spracklin loudly demanded the local police shut down the rampant liquor traffic. The publicity over this brought him to the attention of the Ontario government. He was put in charge of a "flying squad" of liquor inspectors.

For the next few months Spracklin was the terror of the Windsor area. Known as The Fighting Parson, he roamed incessantly with a gang of enforcers and a pocketful of blank search warrants. He fought his way in and out of raids, waving guns and strong-arming suspects. On the Detroit River, his favorite tactic was to ram a suspicious boat with his own. In return for his vigorous pursuit of lawfulness, his home was twice riddled with bullets.

By November, it was all over. Still eager to nab his old nemesis Trumble, Spracklin went too far. He and his men broke into Trumble's place in the middle of the night and, in the confusion that followed, Spracklin shot the unarmed Trumble dead.

Stripped of his inspector's license, Spracklin was tried and acquitted of manslaughter, then tried and fined for one of his

other violent searches. Still later, he was accused of sexual misconduct. He moved to Michigan — and a series of continually smaller churches. He died, aged seventy-three, in 1960.

Smuggling Something Else

In the midst of all the liquor traffic across the Detroit River, a man named Barnet Braverman rode the ferry from Detroit to Windsor every day. Every evening, he too would slip a little something back over the border. In Braverman's case, it was copies of James Joyce's new novel, *Ulysses*, which was banned in the U.S. Over a month or so, he smuggled the first forty copies of the book, now considered a classic, into the States, and then mailed them to friends across the country. Braverman was drunk on words.

Us Against Them

4

Riots and Rebellions

There are lots of ways to disagree. In a democracy, it's a healthy thing — unless people pick up sticks, stones, guns, knives, and pitchforks to make their point.

We polite Canadians have a way with a riot. Back in 1885, vaccinations were ordered during a cholera epidemic in Montreal. The suspicious, stressed-out citizens took to the streets; doctors had to travel with armed escorts. White mobs attacked Chinese immigrants in B.C. early in the 20th century. Quebecers rioted against World War I conscription in 1917 and 1918. Violence engulfed the Winnipeg General Strike the following year. Protestants fought Catholics. The Irish fought the French. The French fought the British. Politicians — and their followers — fought each other. Helped along by lots of free liquor, political meetings turned into brawls, candidates were chased by opposing forces, fights broke out at polling stations. In 1865, two politicians went at it right in the assembly of the Province of Canada.

Still, all of this is a long way from trying to actually overthrow the government. That has happened, too. Whether the people involved were patriots or traitors depends on your point of view. Remember William Johnston? Was he a traitor? He said the government stole *his* property. Here are a few others to think over.

Crème Brûlé

Etienne Brûlé was sent by Champlain to explore and trade with Native peoples in the early 1600s, mainly to build up the fur trade. A free spirit, Brûlé found he loved much of Native life, particularly the girls. This put him in conflict with French priests, but he was too valuable to Champlain to be interfered with. Then, in 1629, with England and France at war, a British privateer (basically, a licensed pirate) attacked French settlements. Brûlé switched sides and guided the English force to Quebec. Champlain had to surrender in return for safe passage home. Meeting Brûlé, he cursed him. Brûlé went back to the fur trade, this time working for the English. Unfortunately for him, when the war ended in 1632, the French got their settlements back. Brûlé was living among the Hurons when Champlain returned. His former boss was not inclined to help when Brûlé found himself in a spot of trouble with his Huron hosts — who killed, cooked, and ate him.

Rebels Without a Pause

By the 1830s, reform-minded citizens in Upper and Lower Canada were fed up with the hard-line rule of a snobbish upper class that didn't want to share power or change with the times. The governing elite were known as the Family Compact.

In Lower Canada, Louis-Joseph Papineau led the push for change; in Upper Canada it was William Lyon Mackenzie. A tiny Scottish spitfire, Mackenzie was the first mayor of Toronto. He also ran a newspaper called the *Colonial Advocate*. Both he and his paper had one volume level: loud. On market days, the red-haired Mackenzie would stand on a wagon and harangue shoppers about the evils of the Compact. His opponents tried to roll the wagon into Lake Ontario while he spoke. Another time, they smashed the printing press in the basement of his house and threw it in the lake. The publicity and cash he got when he sued his tormentors revitalized the paper. (Even people who agreed with Mackenzie tended to get tired of him.) In 1837, both Mackenzie and Papineau decided the only way to change things was by rebelling. Both failed miserably and fled to the United States.

Hunting the Hunters

The immediate fallout of the 1837 Rebellions was violent unrest. The governments began a program of search-and-seizures hunting for rebels and sympathizers. The brutality of the campaign got ratcheted up as two new secret societies struck back. Made up of rebels who had fled across the border, they called themselves the Patriot Hunters in Upper Canada and the Frères Chasseurs in Lower. Neither Mackenzie nor Papineau was willing to join them.

The Hunters specialized in thieving and burning things, and William Johnston was deeply involved (see *It's A Steal*). Apparently, they really thought settlers would flock to join them, but they hedged their bets by being small-time crooks as well. One historian called them "a cross between the Masons and the Mafia." Their wives embroidered some flags for them, and the gang had four membership levels: Snowshoes, Beavers, Grand Masters, and Patriot Hunters. Each one had its own signals. Snowshoes, for example, greeted each other by pinching their sleeves and putting a finger in their nose or ear (no kidding). Beavers gnawed their thumbs. Hunters scratched their snuffboxes.

The Frères Chausseurs were a greater threat, but no more successful, despite widespread hatred of the British in Lower Canada. Led by Robert Nelson, a Montreal doctor, a ragtag band of Frères made two fruitless attempts to march on Montreal in 1838, hoping to connect with underground cells of the movement scattered around Lower Canada. The British conducted a string of savage reprisals. Nelson gave the whole thing up in disgust, returned to the U.S., and went back to being a doctor.

Others weren't so lucky. Some 150 rebels in Upper and Lower Canada were transported to Australian penal colonies; thirty-two men were hanged. The government had intended to hang more, but the executions were so unpopular in British Upper Canada that they backed off.

Traitors or patriots? The right idea and the wrong method? Ultimately, the Rebellions provoked a commission of inquiry led by Britain's Lord Durham. It recommended the union of Upper and Lower Canada under a far more responsible government. The surviving rebels might well have said, "We told you so." A century later, the names of Mackenzie and Papineau were adopted as symbols of liberty by the volunteers of the Mackenzie-Papineau Battalion, Canadians who fought against the Fascists in the Spanish Civil War of the 1930s.

The Tragedy of Louis Riel

Louis Riel was Métis (a people of mixed race, often Native and French Canadian). When Canada bought the North West in 1869, the Métis living there worried about what might become of their way of life. A noisy group of settlers from Ontario was clamouring for a new province.

Riel was young, charismatic, violent — and a Catholic mystic to boot. As a Métis leader, he declared a government around the Red River. If things had gone well, he probably would have

ended up negotiating with the Canadian government and becoming Manitoba's father of Confederation. Unfortunately, before anyone could arrive from Canada (there were no railroads out west back then; travel took weeks), a loud-mouthed Protestant settler tried to kill Riel. Riel had him executed.

Ontario went berserk at the news and offered a $5,000 reward for Riel. A military expedition was demanded. A wanted man, Riel fled to the United States. Even so, his groundwork led to the creation of the province of Manitoba and his followers twice elected him to Parliament. (He never took his seat, but in 1874 he slipped in and signed the Member's register.)

By 1884 Riel was broke and teaching school in Montana. Manitoba had long been a province and the Métis, who had been promised land on joining Canada, were still unhappily waiting. Gabriel Dumont, one of their leaders, asked Riel to come back and help.

Riel was happy to oblige. Unhappily, he was a changed man. Since signing the parliamentary register, he'd also signed the register in a couple of insane asylums. He was having visions and saying he was a prophet. This did not make him a calming influence, although he did hint that he could be one for the right price. At any rate, the Métis pot boiled over into rebellion on March 25, 1885, with a shootout at remote Duck Lake in what is now Saskatchewan. The rebels won.

Riel leaped back into Ontario's headlines. An expeditionary force was instantly organized. It reached the West in the astonishingly short time of ten days, thanks to some spectacular improvising on the part of the incomplete Canadian Pacific Railroad. The feat saved the railroad, which had been teetering on the brink of bankruptcy (the government now had to pay it back with a massive loan), and doomed Riel. Captured, he was tried for treason. After a controversial trial in which his sanity was questioned, he was convicted and hanged on November 16, 1885. What drove the man and what justice he received are questions still argued over today. His image grips the Canadian imagination — and perhaps our consciences — as fiercely as spikes grip the rails.

Louis Riel

Them Against Us

5

The Government Gets Into the Act

Sometimes we turn against the government; sometimes the government turns against us. In Canada, this is rarely with sticks and stones — more often, we get the short end of a different kind of stick. When the people we elect to do things for us do things for themselves or their friends instead, we get cheated.

Most politicians are wise enough and honest enough to steer clear of situations in which their interests are in conflict

with ours. They're supposed to; it happens to be a law. Others just can't resist the temptation. Back in 1672, for example, Governor Frontenac made it a law that French fur traders could not deal with the English. Then he turned around and quietly started dealing furs to the English himself, at twice the French price. In 1849, corruption reached a new, um, low, when it was learned that the warden of Canada's supposed "model" prison at Kingston was a crook himself. He and his family were buying the cheapest, poorest-quality food they could find for the prisoners, billing the government for more and better supplies, and skimming the profits. Clearly, they were in the right place, but on the wrong side of the bars.

Since then, corruption has become something of a Canadian tradition and, according to today's headlines, it's still alive and well.

"Oh, and isn't it tired of voting I am?"

In the 1800s, bribing people to vote for you was pretty much an accepted business expense, as was paying to have the voter's list tampered with — you could add people so your supporters could vote twice under different names, or you could leave off your opponent's supporters. A candidate's helper would be waiting to offer you cash, right at the door of the polling station. Back then, voting was "open," rather than secret: you went in, gave your name, and announced your choice in public. This made it easy to intimidate voters. It also made it easy for politicians to check on whether they were getting value for their bribery dollar. In fact, there was a standing joke in the politics business: my supporters can't be bought like yours — mine cost more.

Confederation itself fell and rose again thanks to bribery. In 1865, the government of New Brunswick called an election to ratify the plan for Canada hammered out by the Fathers of Confederation. Rich investors didn't like it that the plan called for a Canadian railroad; they wanted one to the U.S. instead. In the traditional New Brunswick way, they bought more votes than the government, and Confederation was dead. Luckily for us, there was another election in 1866. This time, Canada's Grand Trunk Railroad gave the pro-Confederation forces enough cash to out-bribe their opponents. They won the election and Confederation was saved.

The Ties that Bind

Railroads were the cutting edge in the 1800s. You had to have them for a country to grow, and they were vastly expensive. At the same time, if there was little or no competition, railroads looked as if they could be hugely profitable. There was a lot of money rolling down the tracks — and into the pockets of some interesting people.

Railroads, especially the Grand Trunk, were big fans of Confederation, because hooking up with the eastern colonies would increase their business. By an odd coincidence, many of the politicians calling for Confederation also had high-level jobs with the railroads. Which meant that every time the railroads were short of cash, they could find sympathetic friends in government to give them public money — taxpayer's money; *our* money — to help out. And then, of course, if the politicians needed a little something come election time, the railroads would have money — taxpayer's money; *our* money — on hand to help *them* out. What a great system! For everyone but us.

Railroad corruption peaked during the building of the CPR and the 1872 election. Caught up in a tight race, the desperate Conservative government of John A. Macdonald and George-Etienne Cartier promised the railroad contract to a man named Hugh Allan, in return for campaign "expenses." Allan paid out $350,000 to buy the election for them. When news of this came out the next year, there was a huge uproar and the government was forced to resign.

The Pacific Scandal, as it was called, damaged everyone — temporarily. A few years later, Macdonald was back in charge and a railroad was being built, thanks to huge infusions of tax dollars. Macdonald knew that if the railroad died, so would the Conservative party, so he moved heaven and earth to keep the cash flowing. The CPR understood its part of the bargain; everyone who worked for the railroad was under orders to always vote Conservative.

The Beat Goes On

If anyone thought lessons had been learned by the CPR mess, they were wrong. In 1886, M.P. Dr. George Landerkin detailed a whole laundry list of Members of Parliament, including cabinet ministers, who had blatant conflicts of interest. Most were connected to railroads.

The arrogance continued. In World War II, C.D. Howe, the minister of Trade and Commerce, approved some spectacularly lucrative contracts for wartime supplies and services, in return

for cash donations to the Liberal party. Howe was happy to go and pick up the cash himself, if necessary. Later, when dealing in stocks while still minister of Trade and Commerce, he cleverly replied to criticism about conflict of interest by saying, "Nuts."

Landerkin, by the way, had also criticized a government member who owned a printing firm that got contracts from — guess where — the government. It was routinely paid for work it didn't do, and vastly overpaid for what it did. Depressingly, a similar scandal was rocking Ottawa over a hundred years later. Some things never change.

Sweet and Sour Swindles

6

It Takes Confidence

Of course, you don't have to be a politician to be good at snaffling other people's money. You don't have to be the bloodthirsty type either. A persuasive voice, an honest face, nimble fingers, and a discreet appeal to the greed of others can be every bit as powerful as a cabinet post or a pistol.

You don't even have to think of yourself as a crook. The stalwart traders of the Hudson's Bay Company were reminded that company policy included cheating the Natives they traded with. Testimony before an 1889 Royal Commission in Montreal revealed the story of a fourteen-year-old who was being paid $1.60 a week for sixty hours work. His first week on the job, he was fined $1.75 for insolence, and the company demanded he pay *them* the 15-cent difference. Clearly there are many ways to turn a profit.

Bytown Blues

You'd think that a priest would be the one person you could trust, but the luckless Roman Catholic parishioners of Bytown would have disagreed. In the 1820s and '30s, Bytown was a rough and tumble mud pit of a place that featured frequent clashes between the Irish and French competing for work in the lumber camps. (Later it would get dressed up and become Ottawa.) The first priest assigned to the parish was the Reverend Patrick Horan, who found saving souls to be thirsty work. In fact, Reverend Horan had such a spectacular thirst that his drinking far outstripped his meagre salary. Nipping from the communion wine didn't help, so he took to selling off church land and keeping the money to buy more liquor. When his real estate ventures were discovered in 1829, he was sent packing. His successor from 1832-35 turned out to have a different problem: he was an imposter, untrained and unordained. True confessions, indeed.

Canada Bill

In the grand tradition of Ben Thompson (see *Mostly Murder*) and "Flat Nose" George Curry (see *It's a Steal*), Canadians who took their talents south to greener pastures, Bill Jones came to fame in the U.S. Known as Canada Bill, Jones was a card shark who coined the phrase "the only game in town." His specialty was riding trains and riverboats, posing as an innocent yokel to lure unsuspecting victims into card games he seemed guaranteed to lose — except that he would always win.

Jones was so spectacularly successful at this that the railways were bombarded with complaints. Railroad detectives kept watch for him in his various disguises, and threw him off trains whenever they could. Rather than giving up, Canada Bill offered the railroads a share of his profits if they'd leave him alone. When they refused, he simply upped the offer. A con man's con man, Jones was so smooth that a fellow trickster was heard to say at Jones's funeral, "Why, I've seen Bill get out of tighter spots than this."

The Answer to Everything

Somewhat less smooth were George and Charlie Tooke, brothers who in 1881 hatched a scheme to get rich quick. In those days, Grade Twelve final exams, called "departmentals," were set for all of Ontario by the Ministry of Education. Students lived in fear of them. The exams were tough, and you didn't graduate unless you passed. The Tookes, no geniuses themselves, were smart enough to know that greed plus wanting to beat the system equal a sucker. They wanted money; students wanted to pass without studying. It was a perfect fit. Charlie, a school teacher, wrote up a set of bogus

exams. George got his hands on lists of Grade Twelve students all around southern Ontario and mailed each kid a letter advertising a chance to buy the "departmentals" in advance. (To give the brothers some grudging credit, it must have been a lot of work in pre-photocopier days to copy out hundreds of letters and exam papers by hand.)

They hit the jackpot. Money rolled in and a small mountain of fake, utterly useless exams were mailed out. The only thing the Tookes didn't count on was that their victims had even more gall than they did. When they found they'd been fleeced, many of the students complained to the police — even though they themselves had been trying to cheat. Charlie was nabbed as he picked up more mail from the post office boxes George had rented to handle it all. The Tooke brothers got six months apiece. What the students got on their exams remains a mystery.

Real Counterfeiters

In the 1880s, the Johnson family was the real thing. They ran their business out of a house in a quiet Toronto neighborhood. Dad was a master engraver, which meant he was an expert at delicately etching lines onto metal printing plates. To do this, you shave away the other parts of the plate so the lines you want will be raised. You also have to do it backwards, to make the plate a mirror image. Then, when the raised lines are coated with ink, they will print a copy that *isn't* backwards. For centuries, master engravers had made high-quality reproductions of pictures and fancy lettering. Mr. Johnson's own, very demanding specialty was high-quality reproductions of money. It was a family affair. Johnson was teaching his sons the same skills. His daughters had been taught how to imitate other people's signatures. His wife handled business matters. Unfortunately, making beautiful copies of money is called *counterfeiting*, doing business with it is known as *fraud*, and imitating other people's signatures is *forgery*. They all happen to be against the law.

For years, the Johnsons moved between Canada and the U.S., faking bills of all sizes. Mr. Johnson kept his printing plates wrapped in waterproof oilcloth and buried in a forest just outside Toronto. Once a year he'd dig them up and print up a batch of money. Then Mrs. Johnson would sell the fakes to a wholesaler for a portion of their face value. The wholesaler would resell it to a "shover," a person who actually put the money in circulation, usually by buying some small item with a large bill and getting real money as change.

Long suspected, the family was careful never to be caught trying to pass the counterfeits themselves — until one night

when Mr. Johnson went on an uncharacteristic drinking spree.
As he got drunker, he began passing low-denomination bills to
finance his evening. By the time the family business was shut
down by the police, it was estimated that about $1,000,000 of
their handiwork was in circulation.

Picture This

Money isn't the only thing worth counterfeiting. Canadians got
the picture in 1963, when the first art-fraud trial in North

America took place in Toronto. Several art dealers in the city were charged with selling paintings that they claimed were by such famous artists as A.Y. Jackson, Emily Carr, and Cornelius Kreighoff, all the while knowing that they were imitations painted to look like the real thing.

Breaking the Banks

Banks have always been popular targets for scams, often run by their own employees. Where else are you going to find so much money just waiting to be taken?

From 1832 to 1871, James Forman, was the chief cashier at the Bank of Nova Scotia in Halifax. Starting in 1844, he squirreled away the then-staggering sum of $300,000 dollars — a dollar here and a dollar there — from other people's accounts. This embezzlement of 15 percent of the bank's total assets was discovered only when he retired. Forman had been a trusted senior employee. It was his job to check others' arithmetic; no one had bothered to check his.

Then there was the Banque de St. Jean, run by Philippe Roy, the Speaker of the Quebec Legislature. In 1908, the bank went belly-up, thanks to some crooked deals Roy had cooked up, losing all the money deposited in it. Convicted of fraud and forgery, Roy attempted suicide by shooting himself in the foot. Oddly, he didn't die, so he was sent to the penitentiary.

Crime paid in a more recent version of Forman's skimming technique. A bank branch discovered fraud when it decided to give a prize to the customer who did the most business there. Surprisingly, the most active account belonged to one of their employees, who was using the bank's computer system to transfer fractions of a cent from other accounts into his own.

(The fractions were generated by precisely calculated interest payments.) By the time he was caught, he'd collected $70,000. The man went unpunished so the bank didn't have to explain to customers that it too routinely rounded off customer's accounts in its favour.

Music to his Ears

In the early 1920s, with sound recording in its infancy, the music business made its biggest money by selling printed "sheet" music. Winnipeg's Joseph Xavier Hearst decided to cash in — not by printing music, but by convincing other people he was going to and that they should invest in his company. With the demand for music, Hearst said, it was guaranteed to make everyone a fortune. To attract investors, he forged purchase orders from the Eaton's department store chain and a letter from the Chase Manhattan Bank that showed it had invested. In two years he hadn't printed a note of music, but he had rounded up a jingly $500,000. Hearst took the money and ran. Inexplicably, he returned in 1925 and faced the music. He was out of jail four years later; the money was gone.

A Stock Answer

Part of the appeal of the stock market is the excitement of gambling, particularly when a stock's value takes off. This often happens with stock shares in mining companies: a big mineral find somewhere, or the rumour of one, can send prices soaring as investors scramble to get in on a good thing. But there are also ways to make prices soar without going to all the trouble of prospecting. Viola Macmillan knew one of them.

Viola's job was to look for investors in mining companies.

Short of a lucky strike, the best way to get people interested was to make a company's stock look like it was in demand, and therefore more valuable. So Viola decided to generate a little action on her own. In July 1964 she sold 244,000 shares of

Golden Arrow Mining stock, re-buying it under another name, to make it look as if lots of people were suddenly buying Golden Arrow. Her trick worked. Demand for Golden Arrow hit the Vancouver Stock Exchange and the stock's price doubled. Viola sold out for a huge profit. She was also convicted of fraud and did some jail time. Selling stock to yourself to create a phony impression of big interest is called "wash" trading. And nothing comes clean out of that wash — it happens to be a crime.

Does Not Compute

The advent of computers and electronic record keeping has made fraud easier to detect, but it has also given rise to some sweetly sour swindles. The most audacious one involved a

Canadian company that was forced to pay off one of its own employees after he hacked into the company's computer system and changed the password to the data bank. For $50,000, he told his bosses the new password, the only way they could get back into their own computer system. Management of the company was too embarrassed to press charges.

Unbeatable Betsy Bigley

Swindlers can be perversely appealing, especially if their victims seem too rich or foolish to care about. There were none better than Betsy Bigley, who conned rich and poor alike until her last scam made her famous. Born in 1857, she ran away from home at age fourteen, opened a bank account in nearby Woodstock, Ontario, and proceeded to write cheques on it with no money to cover them. (This is known as "kiting" cheques). She was caught and returned home, only to run off a year later, this time to Toronto. There she stayed in a luxury hotel, claiming to be a niece of the Cunard family of famously wealthy shipowners, and again kiting cheques to cover her expenses.

Skipping out on her bills, she returned to London and worked as a call girl for several years, romantically calling herself Emily Heathcliff. Then she learned her sister had married and moved to Cleveland, Ohio. Betsy followed and set up shop as Lydia DeVere, clairvoyant. She raised start-up funds for her new life by pawning furniture from her sister's home and disappearing with the money to another, classier part of town.

By 1882, she had captivated a local doctor, who found out about her staggering string of debts only when bill collectors began pounding on his door the day after their marriage.

Divorce proceedings began twelve days later. Undaunted, Betsy moved around to places like Buffalo, New York, and Erie, Pennsylvania, staying in hotels and then skipping out on the bill. On one occasion, she escaped the tab by faking her own death.

Back in Cleveland in 1883, she remarried, this time to a wealthy farmer. He agreed to a marriage contract that more or less gave her everything if they split up. Four years later Betsy cleaned him out and left town for Toledo, Ohio, where she went

back into the mind-reading game. Soon she was fleecing a victim named Joe Lamb, who ended up being arrested for forgery with her when he tried to cash notes from "rich uncles" who didn't exist. Lamb was acquitted when his lawyer used a novel defence: Betsey had hypnotized him. Betsy got nine years.

She served three and a half. When she got out, she began running a brothel in Cleveland, her favourite city. There she met a lonely doctor named Leroy Chadwick. Even better than lonely, Chadwick was wealthy. Betsy convinced him she was an innocent victim — and the illegitimate daughter of the famous steel magnate Andrew Carnegie. Soon she was Mrs. Chadwick.

After running through Chadwick's money, Betsy was ready for the scam that made her famous. She conned a local bank president with her Carnegie story, and he loaned her as much money as she wanted on the strength of a forged note that seemed to be signed by the multi-millionaire. The banker called this note a "security on deposit." Betsy took the receipt for the note to another bank and got another loan, which she took to another bank as security for an even bigger loan....

Everyone believed her. She even took one banker to Carnegie's mansion and left him in a cab outside. She went in, asked the housekeeper if any maid's jobs were available and then returned to the cab carrying an envelope stuffed with newspapers that she'd had hidden under her coat. She told the banker it contained $5,000,000 in securities. Believing she'd just been talking to Carnegie, the banker accepted it without even looking inside.

Betsy cast her net wider and wider with such audacity that no one could *not* believe. She used the money people gave her to make token payments on a few of her debts while continuing to live like a queen. The rest of her debts were put off or simply ignored, until finally a Boston banker sued her for the money she owed him.

When asked, Andrew Carnegie said he'd never heard of her. Betsey was arrested in her hotel suite in New York. The whole story unravelled, and the Carnegie name drew huge press coverage. Betsey was tried and convicted in 1905. Carnegie himself attended the trial; her hapless husband stayed in Europe.

Betsy pulled ten years in the Ohio State Penitentiary where, true to form, she and the warden charged twenty-five cents apiece for people to visit her. She died in jail in October 1907, having already planned her own funeral. Buried in Woodstock, Ontario, the rumour was that she wasn't in the coffin. How could she have missed one last opportunity to pull a fast one?

7

Called the Cops

Crime in Canada didn't occur for lack of laws. Both France and England had law codes that settlers brought along with them, and new twists were added here. In New France, believe it or not, it was against the law to not be married, for kids to play in the street at certain times, and to leave church during the sermon.

What was missing was a police force. Neither France nor England, the mother countries of the colonies, had anything like our modern police. France had a police system that consisted of paid informants (usually servants) who reported to inspectors, who reported to the king. The king could order you arrested by the army and throw you in jail without a trial.

In England, the idea was that everyone helped keep the peace. Anyone could make an arrest. Communities had an unpaid, part-time constable and his assistant, the watchman. People took turns filling the jobs, and it was everyone's duty to help if the constable called on them. If someone got arrested, the constable took the suspect before a magistrate appointed by the king. The magistrate acted as judge, prosecutor, and defender.

If something was stolen, you might go to a "thief-taker," someone who'd try to solve your case for a fee or reward. Usually, the thief-takers were thieves themselves. The most famous was London's Jonathan Wild. Wild was so obviously corrupt that when he was finally hanged, the government decided to replace thief-takers by paying constables fees for solving thefts. This turned into the idea of paid police officers. In 1829, London got the first real police force — meaning officers in uniform, on patrol, and paid a salary. As well as making arrests, they lit street lamps, called the time, and watched for fires. Because the force was created by Sir Robert Peel, the policemen were known as Peelers, or "bobbies."

SIR Robert Peel

Constables of Canada

The constable-and-watchman system was basically what was used in French- and English-Canadian settlements. In New France the constables were known as captains of militia. By and large it worked well. The colonies were small, so co-operating and having a sense of community were important for everyone's survival. Few people knew much about the law, but common sense could be just as effective. In extreme cases, soldiers stationed in the colony could help with enforcement.

The Canadian colonies got their first professional police in 1835, when Toronto created a force based on the London bobbies. Quebec City followed in 1838, and Montreal in 1840.

Undetectable

While their presence helped prevent some crimes, the police couldn't do much to solve crimes. The idea of the detective is very new. Thief-takers like Jonathan Wild didn't solve crime by detection; they used informants, or knew about the crimes because they were the brains behind them.

Without witnesses or snitches, early cops were stuck. In New France, they sometimes compensated for this with the *question ordinaire* and *question extraordinaire.* Suspects who wouldn't confess to the magistrate were asked questions again, this time with boards tied to their legs. Wedges of wood were inserted beneath the boards and gradually whacked deeper and deeper in with a hammer. If the pain didn't make you confess to just about anything your questioners wanted, the wedges would fracture your leg bones and you'd probably be left a cripple. These days, we call this torture, and it's against the law instead of being it.

Elementary, My Dear Murray

Because policing was so limited, the railroads had their own detectives, the kind that tried to hound Canada Bill off the tracks down in the U.S. They relied on printed descriptions of suspects, quick wits, keen eyes, and muscle.

At Confederation, the provinces were given the power to set

up provincial police forces. In 1873, the federal government created the North West Mounted Police (see *In the Right Spirits*), which became the RCMP.

For a long time, the provinces did little. Out in the country, the local constable was all that people could rely on. (Unless you were the Donnellys. Then you couldn't rely on *him,* either. See *Mostly Murder*.) Then, in 1875, the province of Ontario hired John Wilson Murray as Provincial Constable. What started as a one-man police force eventually became the Ontario Provincial Police.

Murray had been in the U.S. Navy during the Civil War, and then became a railroad detective, first in the States and then with the Canada Southern Railroad. For the next thirty years, he was more or less *the* government detective, called in all over the province when cases proved too baffling for local constables. He had an astonishing success rate, and became internationally famous for his work on the Benwell murder case (see *Mostly Murder*). It was Murray who nabbed both the Johnson family and the Tooke brothers (see *Sweet and Sour Swindles*), the latter ending with him wrestling one of the Tookes in a mud puddle.

Inevitably, Murray was compared to Sherlock Holmes. It was a good comparison. Like the fictional Holmes, Murray was daring, keenly observant, and not averse to either trickery or violence. Once, while on a case in the U.S., he went into a barbershop for a shave. As he waited his turn he thought he recognized a suspect he was looking for, a bearded man snoozing in the barber's chair. Murray knew the man he wanted had a scar on his cheek. When the barber was called away, Murray grabbed the clippers, trimmed away a patch of the sleeper's whiskers, and spotted the scar. He nipped out to find the sheriff's office, then returned to find his suspect yelling at the bewildered barber for ruining his beard. Murray lured him to the sheriff, and locked him up.

The main reason Murray was compared to Holmes, though, was his painstaking attention to the details of physical evidence. The Benwell case was solved because Murray noticed drops of blood, traced them to the murder scene, and searched for hours on his hands and knees until he found the tiny piece of evidence that identified the body.

Murray pioneered such techniques as taking casts of footprints, using handwriting analysis, and studying forensic evidence. When four barns were torched near Chatham, Ontario, notes found on gateposts said the arson had been committed by local black people to avenge racial insults. Murray solved the case by first noticing that the footprints around each barn were the same, made by brand new boots. One of the "victims" was wearing suspiciously dilapidated

footwear when Murray talked to him. Surely the man had better boots, thought Murray. He searched the man's house and found a notebook with handwriting and paper that matched the notes on the gateposts. The man confessed that he'd burned the barns for the insurance money.

Other times, Murray called in Professor Henry Croft of Toronto's School of Practical Science. Croft, who gave the first testimony in Canada about arsenic poisoning (see *Mostly Murder*) also helped to solve the Ward murder of 1876. The farmhouse of Mr. and Mrs. Ward had burned down. Mr. Ward had odd-looking burns; Mrs. Ward was gone. Sifting through the debris, Murray began bagging objects to look at, including debris from inside a stove that seemed to have been super-

heated. He took it all to Professor Croft, who identified the stove debris as a mixture of human bone and flesh, and chunks of a mattress stained with blood. Murray charged Mr. Ward with murder. He'd killed his wife and burned her body and other evidence in the stove, then torched the house to cover up the crime. Ward's own burns were self-inflicted. He was convicted.

Murray retired in 1904 and proceeded to collaborate on two entertaining volumes of memoirs that, years later, became the basis for a CBC TV series, *The Great Detective*.

The Scientific Method

While John Wilson Murray was cleverly deducing, science was keeping up with him. Oddly, it took the police, of all people, a long time to recognize this.

The invention of photography led some police departments to begin taking pictures of the faces of people they arrested. Victims of robbery or assault could look at a "rogues gallery" of "mug shots" to see if they recognized anyone. Pictures could be sent to other police departments too. (Murray, though, said that he always did better with a written description.)

In 1877, a British civil servant in India, deduced that everyone's fingerprints are unique. Despite a number of tests that confirmed this, the results were not accepted for years. As late as 1912, a U.S. court still rejected them as evidence.

In 1879, a Frenchman named Bertillon came up with another ID system based on the measurements of eleven different bones in your body. The odds against two people having exactly the same measurements were astronomical. Bertillon's method took nearly ten years to catch on.

Next came the identification of different blood types, and

later ballistics tests to match bullets to the guns that had fired them. In recent years, DNA testing has been added to the arsenal.

In 1914, the first forensic science lab in North America was opened in Montreal. Evidence from all over the continent was sent there for testing. The police remained skeptical. The RCMP didn't start its own lab until 1937.

8

Crime and Punishment

Before European colonists arrived in North America, Native peoples had their own communal forms of justice that varied somewhat from group to group. In general though, Native ideas centered on making up for an offense with some kind of repayment. The victim of a wrong could be compensated with a ritual apology, a valued item, having work done for them, or, in extreme cases, the life of the offender. What was appropriate would be decided within the group.

Colonial justice was very different. If you were arrested, the constable would haul you before the magistrate as soon as possible. Until then, you'd sit in a makeshift jail. The jails were horrible places. You might get bread and water for food. In the winter of 1686, a group of prisoners were left in an unheated jail in New France for a few days. Their feet froze and had to be amputated when gangrene set in.

Fortunately, you rarely spent much time in jail before your case was heard. There were two kinds of courts in New France, seigneural and royal. Your trial wouldn't take long either. The magistrate would act as both prosecution and defence to get to the bottom of things. If he found you guilty, he'd also choose your sentence.

The English colonies had local courts with magistrates and

higher, formal courts called the Court of King's (or Queen's) Bench with regular judges. Death sentences could only be handed down by the high court.

Sentencing was very different too. Instead of the Native idea of compensation, the French and British both emphasized deterrence. The law called for a variety of cruel physical punishments to be administered in public; basically to frighten anyone else who might have the wrong ideas.

Fortunately, sentences were often lighter than the law called for. Remember, this was an informal time and place where everyone had to depend on everyone else. There was no point in turning your neighbour into an embittered outcast — or a corpse. By 1800, English law listed more than 200 crimes that called for the death penalty. They included stealing food.

No Logo

Branding was the punishment of choice for petty crime in New France. On sentencing, your hand would be strapped down where you stood, in whatever passed for a courtroom. A red-hot branding iron would be pressed to the back of your hand, on the skin between your thumb and first finger, and held there for as long as it took you to say "Vive le roi" (God save the King) three times. The mark it left would be in the shape of a crown, or a letter that stood for your crime.

Cat-astrophic

In the English colonies, they preferred whipping, known as flogging. When the French flogged, you'd be tied to a cart and led around the settlement, stopping here and there for a few more lashes. The English preferred a whipping post, right in the

middle of town. You'd be tied to the post and beaten across the back with a cat o' nine tails: a whip made of nine separate pieces of rawhide, with a knot tied into each one, all joined to a short handle. Each lash was like being hit with nine whips instead of one. The standard sentence was thirty-nine lashes. This seemingly odd number came from a passage in the Bible in which St. Paul was lashed with "forty stripes save one." (In 1817, a P.E.I. man stole an axe and was sentenced to three floggings in three places, thirty-nine lashes each time.) If the bloody pulp that was your back managed to heal, you'd be scarred for life.

Taking Stock

Then there were the stocks or the pillory. Conveniently, they'd be next to the whipping post. In the pillory, you had to stand, your head and hands clamped in a wooden yoke. In the stocks, you sat, and it was your feet that got yoked into place.

Either way, while you were stuck, you could count on being pelted with anything from rotten food to, well...

Going, going ...

Gone. Speaking of "reforms," how about Pauper Auctions? In the 1830s, you'd be jailed if you couldn't pay a debt. Taxpayers didn't like supporting the poor, who were often seen as lazy. Thus, in 1837, New Brunswick had the arresting idea of auctioning off the poor. "Habitual paupers" were offered up for cheap labour, and the government would actually pay to get the poor off their hands. Bidders would calculate the absolute minimum it would cost to maintain the pauper while he or she worked for them, and submit that as their bid. The government would pick the cheapest bid and pay that amount to the bidder, who then got the pauper as essentially a slave to be worked to death. The practice was so popular that it continued

in Nova Scotia until at least 1880, when a farmer was convicted of murdering a pauper he'd bid for, who had become inconveniently pregnant.

Blues in the Bottle

Then there was the magistrate in Upper Canada who also happened to own a tavern. He'd purposely sell too much liquor until, inevitably, a brawl broke out. He'd have the fighters arrested and try them on the spot. Besides paying fines, the guilty parties would be sentenced to buy each other a drink, to make up.

Time for a Change

By the 1830s and '40s, reformers were beginning to say that maybe criminals could be made into better citizens instead of just being punished. Rehabilitation instead of retribution meant that fines and jails would replace whips and stocks. A "model" penitentiary was built in Kingston, Ontario. Sadly, though, the jails were so awful and most people so uncaring that the new ways were just a stretched-out version of the good old physical punishment. There was no real prison reform in Canada until after World War II, and even now its effectiveness is debated.

In 1889, the idea of parole was adopted: prisoners could be released early for good behaviour, but misbehaving meant they'd go back to jail. Today there are half-way houses to help parolees re-integrate into society. Are jails breeding grounds for career criminals? Places to learn to be a better citizen? Dangerous and inhuman? Is parole too easy to get? The arguments still rage. Either way, one thing is clear: jail is a place you never want to be.

You Never Can Tell

When magistrates gave way to judges and lawyers and trials by jury, things remained unpredictable. In 1856, George Brogdin, a popular lawyer in Port Hope, Ontario, discovered his wife of two years had run off with Thomas Henderson, an old friend of his. Not long after, he met Henderson stepping off a ferry and shot him dead. Tried a month later, Brogdin was acquitted by the jury, despite the testimony of numerous witnesses who saw the whole thing. The verdict was allowed to stand.

Too Much Rope

If Brogdin had been convicted, more than his career would have been over. The ultimate penalty in Canada, until 1976, was death. Now the stiffest sentence, for first-degree murder, is life in prison with no chance of parole for twenty-five years. In cases where experts feel the criminal poses an ongoing danger and can never be rehabilitated, the convict can be termed a Dangerous Offender and will never be released.

From Confederation to the last executions in December 1962, about seven hundred convicts paid that ultimate price, an average of about seven per year. While they didn't occur often, executions were made even more memorable by being, until 1868, public events, drawing festive and sometimes rowdy crowds...and every pickpocket in town. After 1868, executions took place inside prisons before only a small group of witnesses.

The standard method of execution was hanging which, when properly done, could provide a quick death. The condemned person stood on a trap door built into a scaffold, and a noosed rope was fixed around his or her neck. The other end was tied to a frame above, called a gibbet. When the trap door was sprung open, the person dropped, and their neck was supposed to break instantly as they came to the end of the rope. A good executioner checked the victim's weight to figure out just how far the body had to drop for the neck to break. If the rope was too short, the neck wouldn't break. Too long, and the speed of the drop would rip the victim's head off. If the rope wasn't strong enough, it broke — and they had to do everything all over again.

All of this precision was in the more refined 1800s. Earlier, you were simply driven under the gibbet in a cart, the noose was fixed, and the cart was driven away, leaving you to slowly strangle. Even this was seen as relatively humane: English and French penal codes both provided for burning at the stake, breaking on the wheel, and drawing and quartering a condemned prisoner before execution.

A good hangman was multi-talented. He was also responsible for whippings and pillory work — standing beside you, whip in hand, to make sure you faced the crowd fairly while they threw things. Improvisation was sometimes called for. If a neck didn't break, the executioner was expected to climb aboard the victim to speed things along. In 1816, at Toronto's first public hanging, the condemned man, Elijah Dexter, refused to climb up the steps to the scaffold. No one wanted to mar the dignity of the occasion by dragging him up there. "Please," begged the hangman, "You'll only have to do it once." Dexter still refused, so

the hangman finally put him in a cart and drove him under the rope. Dexter was strangled the old-fashioned way.

For his efforts, the hangman not only got paid, he got the condemned man's clothes and the rope, so he could cut them up and sell them for souvenirs. The body was sold to local doctors. (It was the only legal means of obtaining a corpse for dissection.)

For the truly ambitious, there was the combination deal. In 1829, Thomas Easby was hanged for killing his family. Before his body was dissected, the corpse was skinned. Tanned and cut into pieces, bits of Easby's hide sold for two dollars each.

Monsieur Prieur

Did anyone learn anything from all this brutality? In 1837, Lord Durham commuted the death sentences of some of the rebels to transportation (see *Us against Them*). One of them, Francis

Lord Durham

Xavier Prieur, was transported to Australia, where he served eight years in a penal colony. Eventually, Prieur returned to Canada. He could have been an embittered man. Instead, he became a passionate advocate of prison reform, and in 1875 was appointed Superintendent of Canadian prisons. You really never can tell.

Unsolved Mysteries

9

Everyone Loves a Whodunnit

There are few things as tantalizing as an unsolved mystery. The history of Canadian crime holds a few that have fired imaginations ever since they first hit the headlines. Will they ever be solved? That's a mystery in itself.

The Mad Trapper

Albert Johnson kept so quiet as he moved around the North that he seemed strange, even in a region filled with eccentrics. When he did talk, he usually lied about his activities. The lies themselves were not unusual: trappers and prospectors like Johnson were often secretive. The difference with Johnson was the extremes he went to.

Johnson had been noticed before, but his first run-in with the law was in December 1931, when Natives complained to the RCMP that someone was springing their traplines along the Rat River. This was not uncommon in a time when trapping rights and boundaries were vague. Two Mounties took a dogsled to the area and found Johnson's cabin. When Constable Alfred King went to the door, Johnson stared at him through a tiny window, but refused to speak or open up.

Three days later, King returned with help and a search warrant. When King knocked, Johnson shot him, through the door.

A gunfight broke out. The other Mounties managed to get to King and saved his life, racing twenty hours by dogsled, through minus-forty-degree weather to get him to the tiny hospital in Aklavik.

On January 9, a posse trekked out. The weather was brutally cold. This put the Mounties at a disadvantage because Johnson, in a heated cabin with supplies, could wait them out. He'd also fortified the place with rifle loopholes near the floor. When the Mounties called to him that King was alive and that there were no murder charges, Johnson started firing. After a nine-hour siege, dynamite was thrown at the cabin. Johnson kept on shooting. The frozen Mounties had to give up.

When they returned a week later, their man was gone and a blizzard had covered his tracks. Down south, the story had hit the media. Interest was building. Two weeks of searching finally turned up a faint trail. The Mounties began tracking. It became apparent Johnson was a brilliant woodsman. He was wearing his snowshoes backwards to misdirect trackers; moving in a zigzag to double back and see if he was being followed; snaring game to avoid a giveaway gunshot; building small fires under snow banks to minimize smoke. All the while, he was moving through what should have been impassable terrain.

Finally, though, he risked a shot to kill a caribou. The posse found his camp at the foot of a cliff. They crept in close enough to hear him whistling … and someone made a noise. Johnson dove behind a log and killed one man with a rifle shot through the heart. The Mounties retreated. Johnson somehow climbed the cliff behind his camp and escaped again.

The story caused a sensation in Depression-weary North America. Johnson became a kind of perverse folk hero, single-handedly holding off the fabled RCMP, who "always got their man." Like John Dillinger or Jesse James, he caught the public's imagination as a "little guy" bucking the system. Sales of home radios went up as people followed news updates. The RCMP, humiliated, pulled out all the stops. Radio links were set up with home base. For the first time ever, air support was organized for a search party. A bush pilot flew supplies to the searchers and aided the tracking.

But Johnson had vanished again. Two weeks later, the pilot spotted tracks across the Richardson Mountains. It was supposed to be impossible to cross them solo in winter,

but Johnson had done it, apparently heading for Alaska. The Mounties closed in. A few days later, they caught up to him, this time in the open as he crossed the frozen Eagle River. It was twelve against one, but Johnson blazed away, badly wounding another policeman. Ignoring calls to surrender he was killed in a three-way crossfire.

But who was Albert Johnson? He had no identification. His fingerprints were not on file. His death photo led to a possible alias as Arthur Nelson, a man known in northern British Columbia in the 1920s. Then who was Arthur Nelson? No one knows.

Nor does anyone know why he did it. If he was an ex-con on the run, his prints would have turned up. He had been passive in previous encounters with police, so it wasn't a grudge. The trapline problem was too minor to be the cause of his flight. Had he gone off the deep end after too much solitude? Was he a shell-shocked veteran of the First World War? Did he have a death wish? Then why was he running for the border? One theory was that he was a serial killer, who mistakenly thought he was being arrested for murder. Several men had come to gruesome and mysterious ends when Arthur Nelson had been nearby.

Psychotic criminal or honest man spun out of control? Either way, Johnson's Arctic Circle War with the RCMP lasted forty-eight days and stretched over 150 miles of the Canadian North. All that remains of it is a police file and a hiss of radio static.

The Missing Millionaire

On December 1, 1919, Ambrose Small and his wife Theresa signed the papers that sold their business, the profitable Grand Theatre chain. They deposited a check for a cool million dollars in their Toronto bank account, then attended a lunch for one of Theresa's charities. Afterward, Ambrose bought his wife an expensive bracelet. (Theresa was a formidable person. Ambrose had been especially nice to her ever since she'd discovered he'd been seeing another woman.)

In the late afternoon, Ambrose arrived at the Grand Opera House on Adelaide Street, the flagship of his theatres. There he stunned his cantankerous long-time assistant Jack Doughty with the news that the business was sold and that Doughty now had a job with his new bosses in Montreal. Next he met with his lawyer, E.J. Flock. Sometime after Flock left, Ambrose Small disappeared forever.

He wasn't reported missing for weeks, until a friend named Tommy Flynn went to the Toronto police, saying he hadn't heard from him. Small was well known to the police, both as a prominent citizen and as a longtime member of the city's gambling underworld. Indeed, they knew him so well that they happened to have his Bertillon measurements on file (see *Inventing the Police*).

An investigation was begun. Theresa Small claimed she hadn't worried that her husband was gone because he often left unexpectedly. She was adamant that he was probably at a Florida racetrack with a floozy on his arm. The police weren't so sure.

Further poking around turned up a number of interesting facts. Small hadn't given up his girlfriend from the year before. In fact, he was so busy with various ladies that he'd had a secret boudoir built behind his office at the Opera House. While this indicated Theresa might have a point, none of his bank accounts had been touched.

Something — or rather, someone — else was missing, though: Jack Doughty. Doughty had reported to his new job in Montreal, then come back to Toronto, given his sister a package to hide, and disappeared. The package contained more than $100,000 in bonds belonging to Ambrose and Theresa. Had Doughty argued with Small, killed him, and stolen the bonds? He was a chronic complainer who'd plotted and nursed grudges against his employer for years.

And then there were the rumours about Theresa, a high-profile Catholic in a city rife with Protestant bigotry. It was said that a notice asking for prayers for the repose of Ambrose's soul had been posted in her favourite convent — before Ambrose was reported missing. It didn't help when Theresa said that, if Ambrose were dead, she would give his money to the Catholic Church. Had she had him killed? Theresa had distrusted Ambrose so much that she's checked their business books every day. She'd been furious about his affair too.

The case's mixture of scandal, celebrity, show business, and money made it international news. A huge reward was offered. Private detectives and publicity seekers descended like locusts. The police consulted psychics. Sir Arthur Conan Doyle, creator of Sherlock Holmes, was asked for an opinion.

The alcoholic caretaker at the Opera House claimed that Doughty and Small had been fighting in the furnace room on the fateful night. The police sifted all the furnace ashes in the Rosedale ravine, looking for Ambrose's bones. (Intriguingly, they found a number of human ones, but none that would have fitted the missing Ambrose.) A newsboy claimed Small had bought a paper from him the same night, but it turned out he was mistaken about the date. The famous magician Harry Blackstone claimed he'd seen his friend Ambrose months later in a casino in Juarez, Mexico, but that Small had ducked out before he could speak to him.

Months later, with every lead gone dead, Jack Doughty was arrested in Oregon. He'd been hiding out, working as a bookkeeper in a lumber camp. There was no evidence to connect Doughty to Small's disappearance, and Doughty said he knew nothing. Instead, he was tried for theft of the bonds. Theresa swore they must have been stolen. Doughty maintained Ambrose had given them to him. He was convicted anyway, and served five years. When he got out he ran a service station in Toronto, but never talked publicly about Small again.

When the Grand Opera House was torn down in the 1950s the detective who had led the investigation was watching, in case bones were under the basement floor. Nothing was found. Did Ambrose Small just run away from it all? Did Doughty or Theresa murder him? Did he pay a gambling debt with his life? People claim his ghost walks in some of his old theatres, now restored. Perhaps it has the answer.

The Last Word

Every once in a while, a long-standing mystery is solved. Despite Patrick Whelan's conviction for the assassination of D'arcy Magee (see *Mostly Murder*), doubts lingered. There were no witnesses, and the circumstantial evidence against Whelan was slight. Had he been a scapegoat, the handiest suspect, because of his Irish radicalism?

A shot had been fired from Whelan's revolver, but this was long before ballistics testing. Over the years, the gun and death bullet were mislaid and forgotten.

In 1973, however, they were rediscovered in a corner of the National Archives. The pistol, a .32 caliber Smith & Wesson, was test fired, and the distinctive markings on the bullet were compared with the markings on the one that killed Magee. They matched. Justice had been served after all.

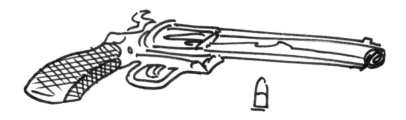

Further Reading

Barrett, Sylvia. *The Arsenic Milkshake*. Toronto: Doubleday
     Canada Limited, 1994.

Boyle, Terry. *Fit to Be Tied; Ontario's Murderous Past*. Toronto:
     Polar Bear Press, 2001.

Butts, Ed, & Horwood, Harold. *Pirates and Outlaws of Canada,
     1610 to 1932*. Toronto: Lynx Images Inc., 2003.

Carrigan, D. Owen. *Crime and Punishment In Canada; A
     History*. Toronto: McClelland and Stewart, Inc., 1991.

Craik, W. Arnot. *Little Tales of Old Port Hope*. Port Hope: The
     Guide Publishing Company Limited, 1966.

Crosbie, John S. *The Incredible Mrs. Chadwick.* Toronto:
     McGraw-Hill Ryerson Limited, 1975.

Gervais, C.H. *The Rumrunners; a Prohibition Scrapbook*.
     Toronto: Firefly Books, 1980.

Hallowell, Gerald (ed.) *The Oxford Companion to Canadian
     History*. Toronto: Oxford University Press, 2004.

Higley, Dahn D. *O.P.P.: The History of the Ontario Provincial
     Police Force*. Toronto: The Queen's Printer, 1984.

Hornberger, Francine. *Mistresses of Mayhem*. Indianapolis:
     Alpha Books, 2002.

Hunt, C.W. *Booze, Boats, and Billions*. Toronto: McClelland and
        Stewart, 1988.

Hunt, C.W. *Whisky and Ice: The Saga of Ben Kerr*. Toronto:
        Dundurn Press Limited, 1995.

Jones, Donald. *Fifty Tales of Toronto*. Toronto: University of
        Toronto Press, 1992.

McClement, Fred. *The Strange Case of Ambrose Small*.
        Toronto: McClelland and Stewart, 1974.

Moore, Lucy. *The Thieves' Opera*. New York: Harcourt, Brace &
        Company, 1997.

Murdoch, Derrick. *Disappearances*. Toronto: Doubleday
        Canada Limited, 1983.

North, Dick. *The Mad Trapper of Rat River*. Toronto: Macmillan
        of Canada, 1972.

Waite, P.B. *The Man from Halifax*. Toronto: University of
        Toronto Press, 1985.

Other Books in the Dreadful Truth Series

The Dreadful Truth: Confederation
By Ted Staunton, Illustrated by Graham Pilsworth
Confederation is a topic no child in school can avoid.
This irreverent and light-hearted book reveals how the fathers
of Confederation engineered their plan and how they used
their newspapers to convince the people. In Charlottetown,
every day was party day as the well-funded Upper Canadians
worked on the reluctant Maritimers at social events. In the
lead-up to key elections, Confederation's friends were quite
happy to use their funds to bribe opponents into silence.
ISBN 0-88780-630-9

The Dreadful Truth: The Halifax Citadel
By Vicki Grant, Illustrated by Graham Pilsworth
Just who would choose to march around Citadel Hill wearing a
kilt in the middle of winter? This book tells you why British
soldiers preferred the icy breezes of Halifax to the palm trees
and sunshine of the Bahamas 150 years ago. This is the first
history book to explain how rank-and-file soldiers lived on 12
cents a day and an endless diet of boiled beef and bread. It
exposes the officers' antics: they had so much status and fun,
they fell flat on their faces after dinner.
ISBN 0-88780-599-X

The Dreadful Truth: Building the Railway
By Ted Staunton, Illustrated by Brian Goff
From the beginning, the railroad business was rife with
scandals, blunders and disasters. In place of the usual tedious
stuff of textbooks, Ted Staunton serves up this history-with-a-
twist, getting at the truth about such things as the railway
developer who blackmailed Prime Minister John A. Macdonald,
and the scramble to build the railway to Manitoba so Louis Riel
could be arrested. And as for the workers who actually built the
railway — this was no national dream. It was a nightmare of
arduous labour, rotten boots, foot fungus and hallucinations.
ISBN 10: 0-88780-690-2
ISBN 13: 978-0-88780-690-2

MEMBER OF SCABRINI GROUP

Québec, Canada
2006